The Text That Made Me Smile

Poems that move around us

Jyotsna Kalkal

BookLeaf Publishing

India | USA | UK

Made with ❤ on the BookLeaf Publishing Platform
www.bookleafpub.in
www.bookleafpub.com

Dedication

Dedicated to
all the kind and loving hearts
striving to make this world a more beautiful and
peaceful place to live in

Preface

Poetry has the power to capture emotions, moments, and unspoken thoughts in a way that lingers in the heart. This collection is a reflection of life's highs and lows, love and regrets, hope and resilience. Each poem is born from deep feelings, quiet observations, and a desire to connect with the soul of the reader.

Dedicated to all the beautiful hearts striving to make this world a kinder place, this book is a tribute to those who love fearlessly, dream endlessly, and find meaning in the smallest of moments.
May these words resonate with you, offering comfort, inspiration, and vibrate as daily reminders to spread happiness.

With love and gratitude
Jyotsna Kalkal

Acknowledgements

This poetry collection is a reflection of the emotions, experiences, and dreams that shape our day to day lives. It would not have been possible without the love, support, and inspiration I have received along the way.

I extend my deepest gratitude to my family and friends, who have stood by me with great faith.

To all the kind souls who bring love, hope, and beauty into this world, you are the true inspiration behind these poems. Your kindness, resilience, and light remind me every day why words matter.

A special thank you to my readers whether you find comfort, connection, or inspiration in these pages, know that this book was written with you in mind. Your presence gives these words meaning, and for that, I am truly grateful.
Thanks almighty!

With heartfelt appreciation
Jyotsna Kalkal

1. The text that made me smile

My heart was cloudy
faith turning fragile
Sunshine with no golden hue
thoughts cluttered in a huge pile
Then glows up the screen
just in a short while
It's the beautiful morning text
that made me smile

2. I choose only you

We fight, we fix
we distance, get mixed
Bored, ignored, shocked, blocked
nerves running fast
Love asking every second
is it going to last?
But it shows up
standing tall and new
Shouting in a million ways-
I choose only you

3. The words will stay

The words you say
will forever stay
You may move further
just forget either
But they are enough
to shatter one's heart anyway
Or add colours to a soul
bind pieces into a whole
Restoring and adoring an effect
that doesn't get swayed away

4. Me and you

I will fight
go wrong or right
But will never
compete for you
If my presence
goes unmeasured
Memories are
not treasured
Let me just walk away
with a short story so true

5. I wish you find time to be happy

In the midst of big plans
standing strong and tall
Fighting newer battles
for success big or small
Chasing every moment
of never ending hurry
I wish you find some time
to be just happy and free

6. Tryst with the self

I don't know when
but some fine day
I sit only with me
just to listen and to say
Apologising for keeping
others in mind
missing every moment
now hard to find
Regretting my absence
at times with whole heart
Getting too busy
for every new start
Pushing my limits
for more and more
Ignoring tired whisper
after and before
I truly feel sad
for not taking care
of this fearless heart
rarest of rare

Sorry for not accepting
the love I was offered
Having sleepless nights
renting out my mind to haunting words
Being available to others
at the time of need
But saying -next time
to self, paying lesser heed
Giving parts of me to those
who don't understand it's value
Learning late to turn to self
hold tight and say I love you
Looking into the mirror
I want to praise and adore
Go dancing on having all that
Others only yearn for
Keeping all the plans
or engagements at bay
I will make it happen
this or that way

7. Don't make me go

Don't make me go
don't close the door
I've found my escape
I need no more
So filled with care
gentle and kind
A peace like this
is hard to find
Don't make me leave
please don't turn away
Let me be with you
just let me stay
If time must move
then let it slow
Hold me close
never let me go
For in this space
in love's embrace
I've found my home
my favourite place

8. I want to be with me

Standing here with
confidence and grace
At peace with
my own embrace
Not looking for getting fixed
wait and see
I just want
to be with me
Shrinking myself
dimming my light
Trying to be at ease
with that's right
I've carried lot of burden
held it tight
Through restless days
and sleepless nights
I want to empty
my cup of pain
Sit all alone in solitude
refresh and rejuvenate the gain

9. Make it now

I don't want to save
things for tomorrow
Love, laughter, happiness
spreading without sorrow
I want to wear
my favorite dress
Not wait for a day
that may come or be less
I want to explore places
try newer skies
meet people, share stories
of joys and cries
I want to glow
the candles bright
Let their warmth
fill up the night
I want to speak
the words I feel
Not keep them hidden
quiet or sealed

Love should be given
time should be spent
Not stored away
in doubts and regret
I want to laugh
without a care
Dance in the sunlight
breathe the air
Use every blessing
feel all shine
Before it fades away
with passing time
So I won't keep
joy locked inside
Waiting for some perfect
occasion or ride

10. It's okay

It's ok if all I did today
was just breathe
Let it be enough
let it be what I seek
No races run
no battles won
yet the sky smiled
the day went on
The earth didn't go reverse
the flowers bloomed right
And I remained
simply in my mind
No great leaps
no grand design
Just steady inhale
and exhale fine
Nothing to revise back
nothing new to show
I am full of fragrance
fresh and ready to go

11. Life moves in it's own way

Sometimes we toil
work hard, giving all
Yet watch our hopes sink
and efforts fall
The seeds we plant
with care and pain
Refuse to sprout
despite the rain
And then, in places
least foreseen
Where hands were
still and fields unclean
A flower blooms
a window opens wide
A gift of destiny
a beautiful turn of tide
Life moves in ways
we can't control
Not every path

will reach its goal
But trust the journey
keep going with the flow
Some joys arrive
when least we know

12. Just listen to me

Just listen to me
whenever I feel low
When sadness rises
and sorrows grow
No need for words
no need to mend
Just be there
like a true friend
No grand advice
no perfect line
No rush to say
it's going be fine
Let silence be
a gentle space
A quiet warmth
a soft embrace
You hold my hand
just see me through

Nothing more than that
you need to do

13. Those little things

Every precious gift
that life brings
I want to enjoy
all those little things
A bird in flight
a smile so bright
The stars that flicker
throughout the night
A sunbeam upon face
and a cup of tea
A hand on my shoulder
some music or poetry
Life is not only found
in huge displays
It should be lived
in each moment always

14. When you bring love

When you bring love
let it be pure
A place to rest
a heart too secure
Not tangled in doubts
not something insane
A guiding star
that removes all pain
Let it bring peace
make things at ease
Make us feel light
like an evening breeze
No heavy chains
no bitter cost
No silent battles
fought and lost
It should not break
it should not bind
But heal the wounds
we often try to hide

15. At times we are joyous

At times we are joyous
next moment feel sad
Soft, caring and light
then lost and mad
Our moods keep shifting
never stand still
Like tides in a sea
against our will
We may be sad
yet hope remains
Like silver lining
in clouds and rain
For joys and sorrows
beautifully intertwine
And light still finds
a way to shine

16. Say it to me now

Just say to me now
whatever you feel
While time is ours
while life is real
Under this sky
on this same ground
Let not a word
be left unsound
No other world
no second start
Just this one chance
to share the hearts
Let silence break
let feelings be free
Speak to me now
before we cease to be

17. Embrace the defeat with grace

I know to embrace
the defeat with grace
To stand unshaken
to hold my place
For every fall
each stumble and scar
Has led me to be
whom I've become so far
I rise, I learn
I face the fight
Not seeking only
victory in sight
For strength is born
in trials I face
I embrace defeat
with regard and grace

18. Keep doing good

They may not say
those words you seek
No claps, no thanks
no voices to leak
Yet good deeds are
not meant to show
It's the light you give
a seed you sow
Do good, though no one
seems to see
Let love and dignity
remain your legacy
So walk your path
stay kind, stay true
The world really needs
more of souls like you

19. Love me with all your heart

Love me with all your heart
If you truly do
With all bright colours
and the golden hue
Don't hold back
don't stand halfway
Be here with me
or simply walk away
I don't need love
that fades with time
A fleeting song
a hollow rhyme
So if you stay
then stay for lifetime
Not dimmed, not shared
show the love that's only mine

20. We start to live

Life seems so small
at once, in just one blink
A wave rising fast
gone before we think
Moments slip by like
sand through hands
Lost in worries, regrets
missed in plans
But suddenly we pause
our minds awake
Realising there is a lot
we can make
Not just to chase
not only to race
But to feel, to love
to give and take
For once we see
how fast time flies
We start to live
before it all dies

21. Unspoken thanks

I may not show it
not always say
But I cherish you
in every way
Through quiet nights
and all long days
You stand beside me
come what may
A friend so true
so calm, so near
Who lifts me up
washes away every tear
In laughter loud
in silence so deep
In secrets only
pure hearts can keep
You've given more than
words only can tell

A bond unshaken
a faith known so well
For standing strong
in every wrong or right
Thanks for making me fearless
and shine so bright

22. Each moment is an impression

Everything comes to us
at its perfect time
So just don't chase things
hurrying and sublime
Enjoy the process
put efforts, make plans
Remember we are here to experience
every dusk and dawn
Each moment is an impression
that will last forever
These will be the stories
making us smile and go crazy ever

* 9 7 8 9 3 6 9 5 3 3 8 3 1 *